Birds of
North America

For Kids

Amazing Animal Books

for Young Readers

By John Davidson

Mendon Cottage Books

JD-Biz Publishing

Read More Amazing Animal Books

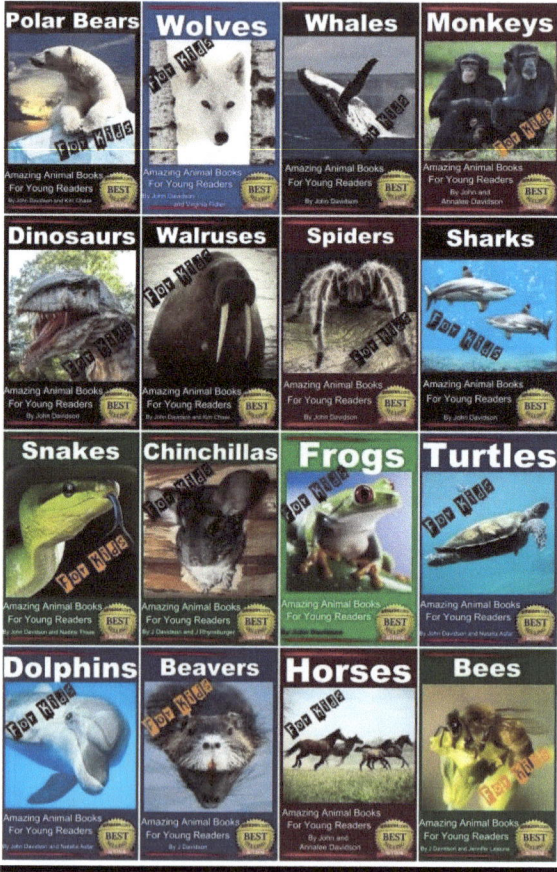

Purchase at Amazon.com

Table of Contents

Introduction

Did you know that some of the birds which people believed would never ever be extinct because they were so numerous have disappeared in the 20th and the 21st century? The last passenger pigeon, which once covered the skies of North America, died in captivity in 1904.

Common North American Bird Families

North America is home to a number of bird species and families. Below, are some of these species.

Anatidae is one common North American bird family. This group includes geese, swans, and ducks. There are a number of types of Anatidae and some are more commonly found in more areas than others. For instance, the Canadian goose is typically found in Canada and the northern states in the US.

Strigidae is another common type of North American bird. The owl is the kind of bird that belongs to this family. In the US, the Snowy Owl is the heaviest owl, followed by the Great Horned Owl.

Another popular North American bird family is the Columbidae. Many people are not too fond of one member of this family, the pigeon. This family does, however, include doves. Many of the birds that belong to this family are found in urban areas throughout the continent.

The penguin belongs to the Spheniscidae family, another common North American bird. Unlike many other birds, this family prefers colder climates. Therefore, they are typically found in Northern Canada and Alaska.

Apodidae is a North American bird family that spends most of its life flying. Their short legs do not allow them to settle on the ground very long. Swift birds make up this family.

Pelecanidae is a popular bird family in North America, but differs from many other birds in that they spend most of their time in the water. Also, these birds have four webbed toes. This group includes egrets, herons, and bitterns.

The Phoenicopteridae family also calls North America home. The bird most people are most familiar with in this family are flamingos. What makes this bird unique from other birds is its height; they can stand up to five feet tall! They love warmer climates, such as the Caribbean Islands and Florida.

Knowing More about the Birds around You – Fun Facts of the More Common Bird Species

All About Blackbirds

Male blackbird.

The Common Blackbird , usually known simply as a "Blackbird ", is a part of the Thrush bird family. Unlike many other birds that are native to just one or two continents, the Blackbird breeds in North Africa, Asia, and Europe. It has even begun to breed recently in Australia. Please do not confuse a blackbird with a crow or with a Raven. They are literally black birds – due to their color – but a common blackbird is a different breed altogether.

The Blackbird typically measures between 23.5 centimeters to 29 centimeters. They usually weigh between 2.8 and 4.4 ounces. Males and females usually differ in appearance. The male has black-brown legs and orange-yellow bill that gets darker during the winter months, and a glossy black plumage. On the other hand, a female Blackbird has a dull yellow-brownish bill, a sooty brown color, and a bit of mottling on its breast.

A male Blackbird is very aggressive when it comes to defending its territory. If they feel as though their territory is being threatened, they do something called a "bow and run." Basically, what this entails is a short run in which the head is first raised and then bowed in quick little jerks. During this time, the bird will dip its tail. When a fight goes down, it is usually a short challenging fight and the intruder is quick to run away.

As far as diet goes, the Blackbird is an omnivore. Their diet includes earthworms, berries, seeds, and many kinds of insects. They usually feed on the ground, running and hopping to grab their food. If they choose to eat fruits, they can grab what is on the ground and will sometimes even go into people's gardens to grab goodies.

The call and song of a Blackbird varies, depending on its purpose. For instance, if the bird is looking to scare away potential enemies, they will make a "*pook-pook-pook* " sound. If it wants to defend its territory from other Blackbird s, it will make a "*chink-chink*" noise.

Unlike many other birds, the Blackbird species is nowhere near extinct. In fact, the population seems to be growing, thriving and multiplying vigorously. This means they should be around for a long time!

Amazing Sparrow Facts

male sparrow.

The most familiar of all birds, sparrows thrive all over the world. The three main groups are the true sparrows, the snowfinches, and the rock sparrows. These are separate and distinct from the American sparrow. You may take them for granted but after reading these facts, you will be amazed at how versatile this bird really is.

1. Sparrows can live just about anywhere.

There have been sparrow sightings in many diverse locations. Entire groups have lived out their lives under the shelter of enormous industrial warehouses.

Cavers discovered a large population 2,000 feet underground in an old coal mine. As long as they can build nests and find food, these birds can make a go of it and survived, even though you cannot find them in the densely populated areas of the Indian subcontinent.

2. Sparrows are notorious for sneaking outside the bonds of monogamy.

Researchers report that up to 28% of all eggs are the product of a female sparrow and a male sparrow who is not her breeding partner. Scientists are puzzled by this behavior. Females with extra-pair offspring have fewer total offspring than their monogamous friends. However, more of the young from extra-pair matings make it to breeding age.

3. House sparrows mostly feed on seeds and other plant matter but in the springtime they can be found busily gathering insects.

Those insects are for the young sparrows. Newly hatched sparrows require more protein and their parents work hard to provide it for them. Living in large flocks, the parents must compete with others for access to the best food for their young. Why this hurry? Sparrow chicks must be ready to fly from the nest within two weeks of hatching.

In some ways, the large sparrow population is due to the progress of human beings especially in the matters of building cities and constructing houses over what was once forestland. They prefer building their nests in man-made structures and love living near their human counterparts. Readily adaptable, they are able to find plenty to eat in the foodstuff we discard or make available to them in our gardens and parks.

Astounding Facts and Information About Hawks

Red Tailed Hawk in flight

A very unique bird that many people have seen throughout their lives is the Hawk. Hawks are a very unique species of bird, one of the most formidable birds of prey in the world today.

Although they may look slightly different, Hawks are actually part of the same family as vultures, ospreys, and falcons. They have the ability to capture their prey, and tear it apart, using their very sharp curved beaks and talons. These birds also have exceptional eyesight, something that allows them to hunt from high above, sighting and pouncing upon their unsuspecting prey below. You have probably seen them soaring above you at great altitudes, something that they can do for long periods of time.

Female hawks are typically much stronger and larger than their male counterparts. Although they are typically reddish-brown on top, and white beneath, they can also be gray in color. You will usually see darker spots or even streaks on their neck. You will see darker bars of color on their wings and tails. Their legs can be feathered all the way down to their toes, and their black talons are very noticeable against the background of yellow feet. In most cases, Hawks can be seen hunting during the day, usually seeking smaller birds or even land animals. There are some species that hunt at night – such as the Bat Hawk – and most of them do not hunt livestock on farms or other areas where domesticated animals are found.

You have probably seen hawks perching on poles or wires, quickly bolting into the air quickly when they see something on the ground. They are capable of making extremely sharp turns even at high speeds, something that makes them very formidable hunters regardless of the location and habitat. Hawks will pounce upon their prey, unless they are able to capture it in midair. In order to stay healthy and active, they must eat at least 25% of their body weight each day.

They can often be seen at the edge of the lake or stream bathing to keep their feathers in a top and sleek condition. Like most birds, they have oil that naturally coats their feathers, making them waterproof and helping them to fly. When they build a nest, they will do so either in trees, or on rocky cliffs to keep their young safe from harm.

Facts About The Cranes

Sandhill Cranes

There are 15 species of cranes. This large bird is found on every continent except in South America and in Antarctica. Their beauty and size have made these birds the stuff of legend and fairy tales. Many members of this species are endangered as the amount of available natural habitats continues to decrease.

1. The Japanese consider the crane to be a National Treasure.

Japanese fables use the crane as an example and symbol of longevity. Legends state that a crane can live for 1,000 years and symbolizes fidelity since cranes mate for life. The Red Crowned crane was thought to be extinct, but a few have been found. Efforts to increase the amount of available wetlands for breeding have been put in place and the numbers are slowly rising.

2. The migratory Sandhill crane is the most common crane in the world.

An omnivorous feeder, the Sandhill crane will eat whatever is available, including tubers, worms, and even snakes. Cranes are fantastic dancers. During the mating ritual, they cavort and sing in unison. Naturally grey with a crimson crown, they are known to apply mud and dirt to their feathers and may appear to be brown.

3. Whooping cranes can reach height of five feet when mature.

Although the Whooping Crane is a flocking bird, there are only two to three birds in a group during migration. They stuff themselves with blue crabs to fatten up prior to leaving for their winter breeding grounds. Birds commonly head for Texas and Florida but a new refuge has been created for them in Louisiana. Their long necks and a wingspan of up to 7.5 feet make them spectacular in flight.

Many cranes are on the endangered species list. The earliest fossil records give an estimated age of ten million years for this remarkable bird. If you ever get the chance to see one in flight, consider yourself lucky.

Facts about the Goldfinch

Male Goldfinch

The Goldfinch is one of the more colorful and gregarious of North American birds. It is a small bird (approximately 5 inches in length) who tends to stand out because of his bright lemon yellow body, white undertail and black wings and cap. Of course, as with a majority of bird species, the male is the more colorful. The female, however, is not without her own beauty, leaning more toward an olive green coloring with touches of yellow and white in her undertail.

The goldfinch generally resides along country roads and in brushy fields and feeds on seeds and grains. He generally can be found in large flocks that swoop and climb the air streams, a treat to the eye for those fortunate enough to run across a flock in flight.

They are social birds, but also territorial when it comes to nesting. They are often found in residential areas and are attracted to bird feeders offering thistle and black sunflower seeds. Once they have discovered your feeders, you are in for a treat! Goldfinches are the ultimate "eye candy" of the bird world!

If you want to attract goldfinches, a good and easily accessible water source is vital, as these birds love a nice bath. Also, in summertime, you might tempt them with a garden offering such treats as Thistle, Coreopsis, Zinnias and berries. Quite often the female returns to build her nest in the same location from year to year. So, if you play your cards right, you will have a friend for life!

A bit of advice about feeders: if you have a lot of squirrels in your yard, go with a mesh feeder. It's harder for squirrels to master, whereas they will destroy the plastic tube type feeder. Also, clean the feeder out after a heavy rain or the goldfinches will not return to it.

Facts and Information About Ducks

You have probably seen ducks flying by, or floating in the water at a nearby pond in your area. There are many different breeds of ducks, coming in a wide variety of colors. Finding information about these wonderful animals can be a rewarding experience, something that you can do on your own, or as a project done with friends and family. If you are interested in ducks, and would like to know a little bit more about them, here are some quick facts about ducks that you ought to know.

Depending upon where you live, you have probably seen ducks in both freshwater and in salt water settings. This is because they can be found in both. These wild, and sometimes domesticated, web footed birds are very common in many places, usually possessing very short legs and depressed bodies that are designed for both flying and swimming. Part of the Anatidae family, these beautiful birds have many different species, but can be easily divided between sea ducks and river ducks. More specifically, they can be further subdivided into South American, Muscovy, China, and wood ducks.

Ducks can live from three years all the way up to a couple decades depending upon their species. They weigh between 7 and 9 pounds and can grow up to 20 inches in length. They have a traditional diet of worms, insects, fish, grass, and even certain tree leaves.

Most duck species are monogamous, only breeding once a year. If you look closely, the wings of a duck are very pointed and short, giving them great strength for both long and short distance flights. Male ducks are called Drake. Females are simply referred to as a Duck. Baby ducks are, of course, called ducklings, and when a large group of them together is called a Brace. This cursory overview of ducks should help you get a better understanding of this beautiful bird.

Muscovy ducks

Domesticated ducks are rather silly birds. Many of them have this bad habit of laying their eggs in the water, – especially if they have been swimming throughout the day – or in really inaccessible places like under shrubs or in brushwood. So if you are raising ducks as providers of eggs, you need to make sure that they have places on land where they can they can lay their eggs. After that, they can be released to swim in the pond.

Facts and Information on Blue Jays

Winter Blue Jay

Blue Jays are a fairly common sight in North America, but that doesn't make them any less interesting to those fond of watching birds. Their cleverness is legendary. They are adaptable and intelligent birds, capable of imitating the sounds of many of their feathered contemporaries.

They are capable of outwitting them as well. Blue Jays are notorious for stealing eggs from the nests of other birds, as well as their nestlings. As humans, that doesn't register well on our sympathy scale, but it's the way of nature and serves to keep things in balance. And don't forget, even blue jays have their share of predators to fear.

Blue Jays are attracted to acorns, nuts and seeds, as well as small critters such as grasshoppers, caterpillars and beetles. If you live in a wooded area and feel you're being swallowed up by the forest, you have Blue Jays, in part, to thank for it. They are hoarders of acorns, but have a tendency to transfer them somewhere - like your front yard - and then fail to retrieve them. The result is a yard full of oak trees you hadn't planned on, blocking your view and preventing the sun from getting through.

There are over 40 species of Jays worldwide, eight of which are common to North America. Many consider the "Jaybird" more of a pest than anything else, but it can also be a big help in ridding your yard of pests. It's fun to watch a blue jay at your bird feeder rigorously shaking the peanuts you have put out to determine which shells still contain nuts.

Blue Jays do migrate in the winter, but this is not a consistent pattern. Some winters find them toughing it out in the snow and cold right along with the rest of us. Scientists as yet have found no explanation for this phenomenon.

Facts and Information on Chickadees

Black-capped Chickadees (poecile atricapilla) on a branch

Chickadees may be one of the more commonly known of the North American birds, but there is nothing "common" about these charming creatures. In fact, you'll have a challenge ahead of you if you want to check off all the different species of chickadee from your life list. Several to watch for are the black-capped chickadee, the Carolina chickadee, the Mountain Chickadee, the Boreal and the chestnut back chickadee.

Most chickadees nest in the cavities of trees and bushes, and are especially fond of rotten or decaying wood. But, the lazier among them aren't above poaching an old woodpecker hole or a "pre-owned" nesting box! The mountain chickadee may even choose a hole in the ground or crevice in a rock formation as his home.

If you want to attract chickadees to your feeder, load up with sunflower seeds or sunflower hearts. You might also offer them some chopped walnuts. You can even hand-feed these little guys. Just stand close to the bird feeder and stretch out your arm with palm flattened and an offering of seeds or nuts. Then wait very quietly. Your patience will be rewarded with a very quick but satisfying visit from your dinner guest. In and out like a puff of air touching your out-stretched hand.

But chickadees are very self-sufficient little creatures who get only about 20% of their winter food from feeders. The rest they find by foraging in the foliage of bushes and trees for spiders and larvae.

Some chickadees, such as the Mountain Chickadee, are only found in the West and particularly - you guessed it - in the mountains (the Rockies to be exact). The Mexican Chickadee is indigenous to New Mexico and Arizona. But wherever you live, you can count on enjoying visits from at least some species of Chickadee.

Facts and Information on Egrets

Great Blue Heron Ardea herodias - Fort Myers Beach

If you have ever seen one of these majestic creatures floating gracefully through the air, you will understand the attraction of the Egret. You will find these large white birds with their long wing-span mostly in wetlands and marshy areas, such as the swamps and marshes of North and South Carolina. Nevertheless they are water birds, and are attracted to most any habitat that offers a decent water source.

Egrets share their habitat with other birds attracted to a watery environment, such as blue herons. In fact, they are a part of the heron family.

There are several types of egrets, Great White Snowy and Cattle Egrets. They build their nests in trees and gather with other wetland birds in colonies. An egret launching itself airborne, stretching its great wings to their full length, is a sight to behold!

The egret's elegance and tenacity to survive made it the perfect symbol for the National Audubon Society. It wasn't that long ago that these beautiful creatures were facing extinction due to the great demand for their large white feathers by the fashion industry. In the late 19th century one could see more of the egrets' beautiful plumage in ladies' hats than on the bird itself. Peacock and ostrich tail feathers plumes have also been much in vogue.

Only 5% of the egret population remained when legislation was finally enacted to protect this lovely creature from extinction! Thankfully, egrets are now once again plentiful and will remain so with proper monitoring and continued protection.

Their diet consists mostly of fish, which they skillfully hunt in their wetland habitat by standing or wading through shallow water to catch unsuspecting fish with a quick jab of their long yellow bills.

Egrets are easy to identify with these bills, their long necks and soft white plumage. An outing to the tidal wetlands of the Carolinas will pretty much guarantee a sighting of these lovely creatures.

Facts and information about Vultures

Endangered California condor flying

When you want to learn more about the many birds in the animal kingdom, the vulture is not a bad place to start. You can learn many facts and get more information about vultures, so that you understand their habits and what they are all about. If you have watched television or read any story involving vultures, they're probably depicted there as an omen of death. This is because they are carnivorous and often scavenge for meat, rather than doing any hunting themselves. For this reason, they circle above when an animal has died or is about to die. These birds typically live on off of this carrion, rather than gathering their own food. They are also found on all the continents on the earth except for Antarctica and Australia.

They tend to stick to themselves, as opposed to congregating in large groups. They are also known for their strong senses, particularly a strong sense of smell and sight. They are thorough when it comes to stripping other animals for food, as they often do not leave any pieces behind except the bones. When you want to learn more about these birds, you should find a source of information in your local library or on the Internet that gives great details about them.

If that is what you were looking for, a good biology Journal is a good place to start. A lot has been written about these birds, and their unique abilities. If you are a bird lover or just someone who loves learning more about animals, this could be a keen endeavor for you upon which to embark. Vultures have had a bad reputation down the ages, so that many people do not know much about them, but if you're looking to learn more, you should make sure that you take advantage of the plentiful information that has been written about them. This will provide you with what you need when you want to know more about this tough and adaptable bird.

Fun Facts About Falcons

A falcon perched on its trainers hand

Falcons are found all over the world with more than 60 known species of this bird of prey. Commonly confused with hawks, falcons have long and pointed wings built for speed and aerial maneuvers. Their bills are notched instead of smooth like the bill of Hawks. Here are some amazing and fun facts about falcons to share with your friends and family.

1. Gyrfalcons are able to live and hunt in Arctic regions.

The gyrfalcon is the undisputed royal bird in the falcon family. The largest of all falcons, it could only be used by a king in the hunt. This fabulous bird lives in cold areas and can be found nesting in Arctic areas. In some cases, gyrfalcons lay their eggs in freezing temperatures.

2. Faster than a speeding bullet, the peregrine falcon has been clocked at speeds of more than 200 mph during a dive.

A Peregrine Falcon (Falco peregrinus) perched on a stump.

Unsurprisingly, this bird is a great hunter and was once the most common daytime predatory bird in the world. As habitat has changed, peregrine falcons have moved to the cities. Commonly spotted flying around skyscrapers, they hunt pigeons and other small prey. Populations of this raptor are growing and it is no longer on the Endangered Species List.

3.   The Merlin is also known as a pigeon hawk.

Falcons and Merlins were tamed by the aristocracy during medieval times. Many tapestries have ladies carrying Merlins on their leather – gloved hands, while riding out on a hunt. Ladies of the European courts frequently flew the trained Merlin during the hunt. Resembling a pigeon during flight, it is smaller than the peregrine falcon and almost as fast. This fierce bird is in constant motion and rarely glides. It patrols open spaces such as meadows and shorelines to find small birds and even dragonflies on which it feeds.

Falcons are incredible hunters and have been used for sport for many generations. Their keen intelligence and hunting skills are appreciated by all who watch them soar through the air.

Fun Facts and Information about Gulls

Herring Gull

One of the most beautiful birds – and among the noisiest –that you will ever see is a seagull. Also known as gulls, these very clever birds can be seen both inland, and most commonly near coastal regions. They have many unique characteristics that set them apart from typical birds that you have probably seen flying by. Here are a few fun facts about gulls that you might find interesting.

A very unique characteristic about gulls is their wide range of feeding habits. Although you will often see them diving into the waters to capture an occasional fish, they are much more clever than you would expect. For instance, if they are able to get a hard shelled mollusk, they will actually take it several yards into the sky, dropping it onto rocks in order to break it open. They also may be seen in fields that have recently been plowed, finding upturned grubs that are one of their favorite sources of food. They may even stomp the ground, imitating rainfall, tricking earthworms to rise to the surface.

Gulls are one of the few birds that can actually drink both freshwater and saltwater. They are born with special glands above their eyes which allows them to flush the salt from seawater that they drink. They are also known to have the ability to communicate with each other, using both body movements and vocalizations that are some form of communication. When they mate, they mate for life, and actually take turns to incubate their eggs. Although they look very similar, there is a considerable amount of diversity between the different species of gulls. Some of them are very small, reaching only 1 foot in length. The larger ones are between 2 and 3 feet in size, weighing almost 4 pounds each.

They are also able to conserve their energy by gliding, and absorb energy from paved roadways during the cold seasons. They are also very fond of crickets, and have been represented by both the settlers of Utah, and Native Americans, as symbols that represent both versatility and freedom. These dynamic birds are definitely unique, possessing both beauty and dynamic qualities in order to survive and flourish.

Information and Facts About Finches

Zebra Finches

Finches are little birds belonging to the same Passeridae Group as the Sparrow and it is easy to miss spotting them, yet they are among the most popular, the most widely observed, and the most popular of pet birds in the world, especially Gold Finches. Many people would rather have a finch as a pet than a parrot or a parakeet. There is much to learn about these tiny, little happy birds.

While it is a fact that most pet birds, such as parrots and parakeets need some kind of human socialization in order to thrive in captivity, finches would rather have the company of other finches, and as far as those humans go, they could take them or leave them. They should be kept in pairs or in groups, and if they are kept individually, they can get physically and mentally unstable, to the point of becoming depressed.

It is customary to handle parrots and parakeets, but not finches. Finches would **rather not be handled** and they should be touched as little as possible to avoid causing them stress and frightening them. So handle the Finches as little as possible to keep them happy.

Finches are among the smallest of the small birds, only weighing less than an ounce and measuring less than 4 inches from beak to tail feathers. While some people might think that this small bird would be the perfect bird for small, cozy homes, quite the opposite is true, as you might need a bigger cage for Finches than for Parrots. Finches have to be able to fly, and the more the merrier. They really need a larger area in a cage to enable them to fly around.

Finches love to sing and chirp, but their tiny voices are so faint they make good choices for people who live in small houses or apartments. Their happy chirp cannot even be heard outside of the room in which they live, and people who have them enjoy their pleasant, happy voices.

Interesting Facts and Information about Owls

Owls are nocturnal predatory birds. This particular bird genus and species belongs to the bird Order – Strigiformes. A nocturnal predator like an owl likes to hunt for its prey at night.

There are two kinds of owls, barn owls and true owls. True owls have about 190 species while there are only about 16 species of barn owls.
Here are some more interesting facts about owls.

Owls cannot move their eyes very much. For this reason, they have developed the ability to turn their heads completely in order to see well. Owls' eyes face forward, so they must use their enhanced sense of binocular sight to find their prey, which includes mammals and insects. Some owls enjoy hunting fish.

Owls are flight birds yet they fly in a silent manner. This is due to the heavy structure of their feathers. Also, the fact that owls hunt mostly at night contributes to their quiet flight. They intend to catch up with their unaware prey which does not know anything about their silent approach and swoop.

Owls –like all other birds-have no teeth with which to eat or chew their prey. They swallow their prey whole. They use their talons, or claws, to clutch and kill their prey. After about six hours, they will regurgitate some of their food, and use it to help make nests, among other things.

It is important to know that owls do not actually make their own nests. They make use of nests made by other birds. Owls come in colors like brown and tan, but they tend to become whatever color their surroundings are most of all. They need to blend into their surroundings in order to camouflage themselves from the prey that they seek.

Owls are found in every continent except Antarctica. When an owl is part of a group of owls, that group is called a parliament. A Parliament of owls! Amusing choice of words, if taken literally.

Barn Owl

Some Basic Facts and Information about Doves

Doves are birds that come in several different closely related species. The most common in the United States and other parts of the North American continent is the Mourning Dove. Next to the Mourning Dove are the Inca Doves and White Tipped Doves in terms of similarity.

Another very common close relative to the dove is the Rock Pigeon, one of the most ubiquitous birds around. Rock pigeons are larger and weigh more than the average dove which weighs up to 6 ounces.

Doves generally have a plump body with a long tail. Their small heads and short legs stand out due to their size in comparison to the rest of their bodies. In North America, the dove's long tail is unique. Doves populate both urban and suburban areas, but stay away from deep wooded areas. In urban and suburban settings, they enjoy using telephone wires as perches.

Doves have a familiar cooing sound. The Mourning Dove is easily identifiable by his or her gentle "who-who-who" call. All doves are swift when it comes to flying. They make steep dives and ascents using their powerful, pointed tails to power their maneuvers.

Doves come in an array of colors. Most all doves have grey feathers, with different markings on their wings such as dots of black, white and dark grey. Doves match their outer surroundings, so they are often found with brown feathers that match nearby trees.

Doves are best enjoyed in their natural settings, but it is all right to invite them closer with scattered millet seeds on the ground. Be generous, because doves eat up to 20% of their body weight each day. In the wild live, doves live a few years, while those in urban areas live to about 11 years of age.

Orioles: Not Just Ballplayers From Baltimore

A female Baltimore oriole bird

The oriole is a beautiful blackbird that's been living alongside humans for centuries. The name is shared by two distinct families of birds, one in Europe and one in the Americas. Below you'll find a little quick information about the orioles that live in the Western Hemisphere.

* Where to Find Orioles

Of course, it's not a coincidence that the baseball team in Baltimore is named after the oriole. Although there are different species living throughout North (and even South) America, orioles are most common along the Atlantic seaboard. In areas with cold winters, orioles are strongly migratory: they'll leave their warm-weather nesting grounds behind when the temperature begins to dip. Further south, though, orioles don't travel quite so much. Wherever you are, your best chance of finding orioles is to search forested areas during the late spring and summer.

* What Makes Orioles Interesting

Orioles are some of the most visually impressive birds in the wide-ranging blackbird family. They have a distinctive, arresting pattern of bright feathers along their undersides. These brightly-colored areas also reach up around the birds' shoulders. The precise color varies with species and sex. Males are usually more vibrant, tending to brilliant yellows and oranges. Female orioles usually have less intense coloration. The females are still worth watching, though! In the beginning of the warm season, female orioles become extremely industrious. They build distinctive hanging nests on the ends of tree branches. Orioles have a notable family dynamic; after their eggs are hatched both mother and father help raise the baby birds.

Orioles are very rewarding subjects for the casual birdwatcher. They're not hard to find, but they are both beautiful and fascinating. If you're interested in seeing orioles for yourself, you can probably locate some with a minimum of effort.

Learning Facts and information about Sandpipers

Least sandpiper, Calidris minutilla

People that love learning about birds have plenty of resources in front of them to help out. No matter what kind of bird you are thinking of learning about, make sure that you look into information about them, so that you're able to do what you need in order to collect and compile all of the necessary information. Regardless of what information you are searching for, it's important to keep up with these particular species', so that you can learn all you can. The sandpiper is a type of bird that usually floats or wades by the shore of oceans. They have wing tips that lead to their tail, and are typically found on a seasonal basis. They migrate to different areas, but always gravitate toward bodies of water. They also have shorter bills than other birds, and are usually more vocal when in flight than when they are on the ground or in the water.

Want to learn more about these birds, research it from a site that provides information about them. There are plenty of encyclopedias, journals and other literary works that have been written to discuss the nature of these birds. Sandpipers are found all over the world in different climates, and they usually stick to water more often than that. We want to find out more about them, be sure that you do your research and learn all that you can about them. This will provide you with what you need in order to learn all about them, and you'll be able to be armed with information about them whenever you need it. The next time you stop by the beach, you will be able to point out these birds and understand fully what type of creatures they are, and will have the knowledge to back it up.

Learn All About Eagles

One of the most majestic kinds of birds in the world is the eagle, part of the Accipitridae family. Africa and Eurasia has the most eagles, where more than sixty species can be found. There are two kinds in Canada and the Unites States, the Golden Eagle and the Bald Eagle. There are three species in Australia and nine in South and Central America.

The eagle is one of the biggest kinds of birds around. Only the vulture has bigger birds than the eagle species. Their long, broad wings makes flying an enjoyable part of these birds' lives. Eagles have long, hooked beaks, making it easier for them to tear apart their prey. Also, this bird is known for their excellent eyesight; Incoming light is usually not scattered because of their great vision.

What an eagle eats varies, depending on the genus. Asian and Africa eagles, for example, enjoy preying on snakes. Bald eagles, on the other hand, like to grab fish out of the water of rivers and streams. However, eagles usually do not land when grabbing their food; it makes it easier for them to fly away with their prey, perch, and tear it apart. Due to their power and size, eagles tend to rank at the top of most food chains.

In 1967, the most common eagles in the United States, the bald eagle, was put on the endangered species list. To this day, there is no clear cut answer as to why bald eagles were considered endangered. Some believe the decline in population began when the Europeans came to the Americas and started hunting. The food they would hunt for is the same food the eagles would eat. Therefore, the eagles would starve to death without their food. Thankfully, the bald eagle was taken of this list in 2007.

Bald Eagles

The American bald eagle is the national birth of North America. Surprisingly it is not bald at all! This is because the world bald actually meant white and this huge bird of prey has a signature white head and neck with a blackish brown body and a white tail. Their beak is sharp and scary looking and at the tip it has a hook which is used for tearing flesh and it can also be used as a weapon. Their talons kill their prey with their talons and they can pen and close them at will.

As with many birds, the male is slightly smaller than the female whose body length can vary from 35 to 37 inches and their wingspan can reach 90 inches. The male is a much smaller 30 to 34 inches but still has a wingspan up to 85 inches. An average bald eagle weighs in at ten to fourteen pounds. They can lift up to about four pounds. While these amazing birds can live up to thirty years, on average their lifespan is around fifteen to twenty.

While half of the bald eagles in the world live in Alaska (35,000) and 20,000 in British Columbia, Canada, the rest can be found everywhere in North America, including northern Mexico. They love the North West coast of America because this is where they can feast on salmon. Fish, alive or dead are an important source of food for all bald eagles. For this reason they are often found where there is water – either along the Pacific coast or on lakes or rivers. They are carrion birds and will feed on creatures that are dead or decaying.

Scientifically speaking bald eagles are actually a sea or fish eagle and there are two subspecies. The southern bald eagle resides in places which are south of 40 degrees latitude. This means Texas, Southern California, the Gulf States as well as South Carolina and Florida. Bald eagles that can be found north of this latitude are the northern bald eagles and they generally veer towards the North West. This eagle is a little bit bigger than its southern counterpart.

Their eyesight is sharp and at least four times as much as a person with perfect vision. Their eyes are quite large – almost as large as ours. They have a high pitched cry even though they have no vocal cords. Their sound is produced in a bony chamber called a syrinx. They use their shrill calls to warn other eagles or predators that this area they are calling from is defended by them.

Why Everyone's Kingfisher Is Different

The kingfisher is a bird with a rich history in many different human societies. It has mythological and cultural significance all over the globe. Besides playing a role in the myths and legends of many different cultures, these clever little carnivores are quite fascinating in their own right!

* Distribution: Everywhere!

The wide-ranging kingfisher family has spread to nearly every part of the globe. From the Americas to Europe to the most remote Pacific Islands, virtually everyone has a local species of kingfisher to call their own. Arctic climates and extremely dry deserts are the only places the kingfishers avoid. This vast range has led to a lot of differentiation; there's a shocking variety of different looks and behaviors within the expansive family of kingfisher sub-species.

* Diet & Behavior

Of course, the very name of the kingfisher suggests its main diet and nesting ground. A majority of kingfishers live close to water and feed on small fish, but there are too many exceptions to make this a real rule. Kingfishers are also found in drier, forested regions. Many species live on insects, lizards, amphibians, or even other birds! Most of the birds in the kingfisher family are burrow-dwellers; rather than building nests they prefer a cozy, well-protected hole.

* Conservation

Although the world has tremendous numbers of kingfishers, human development has put some of them at risk. There are a number of endangered kingfisher species. Kingfishers that have migrated to isolated islands and become adapted to their environments are especially vulnerable. Besides losing habitat space to humans, many of these island kingfishers are severely threatened by invasive species introduced by man.

Like many bird families that are widespread and (mostly) common, the kingfishers are easy to overlook. Ignoring them does them a disservice, though: A little attention easily reveals them to be as fascinating and captivating as many rarer birds!

Useful Facts and Information on Woodpeckers

Male Pileated Woodpecker Dryocopus pileatus on a Dead Pine Tree

The woodpecker is one of the more interesting of the feathered creatures among us. They're also some of the most colorful. If you have bird feeders or live in a wooded area, you no doubt know the joy of sighting one of these majestic creatures.

There are a number of species of woodpecker and many of them share in common some sort of distinctive red marking on their head. This may be confusing, especially to newer birders who aren't sure which of these "redheads" is in fact the genuine "red-headed woodpecker." At least east of the Rockies it's easier to differentiate in that the genuine redheaded woodpecker is the only woodpecker with a FULL red head stretching from his crown all the way down to his pretty little neck.

You may also see Flickers. These smaller woodpeckers can be identified by their zebra-like stripes and, again, a small but distinctive patch of red at the base of its crown. This is not to be confused, however, with the red-bellied woodpecker whose belly is really not all that red, more of a blush of pink. His head, on the other hand, is crowned in red, like a little red Mohawk (as opposed to a full red head). Like the Flicker, the red-bellied woodpecker's body is striped in black and white.

Then there is the bird who inspired the creator of Woody Woodpecker - the pileated woodpecker. He's easy to pick out in a crowd, party because he's simply enormous - the size of a crow! But he also has that distinctive and very large pointed hammer head. It's red also, but more in the shape of a pointed pompadour. One look at his long beak tells you he's ready for business!

Woodpeckers are fascinating and great to watch. Just keep them away from your house or they'll have it looking like Swiss cheese in no time!

Roadrunners

One of the most interesting species of birds is the roadrunner. It is a bird that is black and brown in color, very slender, with a very distinctive head crest. It has a dark oversized bill, very long legs, and has a tail with white tips on three of its outer tail feathers. Another unique feature is the blank patch of skin which is located behind each of its eyes which is red or blue in color. It is a terrestrial bird that can actually fly, yet it spends most of its life running along the ground. If you are lucky enough to see one fly, you will see that the wings are rounded and short, revealing a white crescent created by feathers on its wings. It is a member of the cuckoo family, having only two toes in back and two in the front, something that is technically called zygodactyl feet. Although it can escape predators by flying away, it is more likely to see a roadrunner running at speeds of almost 20 miles an hour to escape any danger.

If you live in the desert regions of the United States, and to even out as far as Missouri or Western Louisiana, you have probably seen these birds running around. Although most of birds tend to focus only on worms and insects for food, roadrunners will eat crickets, lizards, bird eggs, snakes, scorpions and even hummingbirds. It may be because of their excessive running that they need an extremely high protein diet in order to survive. Many people will put up hummingbird feeders, not to feed the hummingbirds, but to attract roadrunners if they are in the area.

There are many other interesting aspects of the roadrunner including the fact that it will secrete excess salt that is in its bloodstream through salt glands located at the front of its eyes. As long as roadrunners eat enough food with high water content, it can actually live for quite some time without drinking water. Roadrunners are also able to expose the skin on their back by fluffing their feathers, allowing them to absorb heat from the sun so that they can survive cold desert nights. Also, despite the popularity of the roadrunner cartoon, it does not make a "beep beep" noise, but something more similar to a cooing sound. If you live in the southwestern United States, northern Mexico, or if you ever visit Baja California, you should be able to see a roadrunner passing by.

Canadian Geese

Canadian Geese are a species of geese, distinctive by a black neck and head, a brown body and white splotches on the face. These birds are native to cooler climates of North America, although they've been found to migrate as far away as Europe. Branta Canadesis was popularly described in Sytema Naturae by Carl Linnaeus, although its first reference dates back to 1772.

The Branta genus predominately describes geese whose feathers are mostly black, separating them from the grey-colored plumage of the Anser genus. The Canada goose has a distinctive trait that differentiates it from all other species of geese world-wide. It has a white "chin strap" that is distinctive on it's black neck and head. The Barnacle goose also has a chinstrap, but it's chest is black and grey plumage on the body.

Canadian geese have several different subspecies making up the genus as a whole which vary in size and coloration, but these seven subspecies are all distinctly Canadian geese. Canadian geese can be anywhere between 30 and 43 inches long, and it's wingspan frequently ranges between 50-73 inches. Males and females are roughly the same size, but males weigh slightly more than their female counterparts and often display aggressive tendencies when defending their territory and breeding ground. Male and female Canadian geese are virtually indistinguishable in coloration and plumage, yet they make different sounding vocalizations.

Canadian geese often breed and are found in the Northern United States, and there is a large population to be found around the Great Lakes in particular. Canadian geese that make their home on the Pacific Coast as well as the Eastern seaboard often stay there year-round as the temperature fluctuations are more moderate than in more northern climates. Canadian geese often migrate to California, South Carolina and even Mexico in the winter months.

Canadian geese were over-hunted between the 19th and early 20th century, and as a result their numbers significantly dwindled. In fact, a large number of researchers believed the Giant Canada Goose was extinct for a time until a small population was discovered in Minnesota. Breeding facilities began monitoring these birds and their populations, and they began successfully breeding pairs to ensure their survival. over 6,000 giant Canadian Geese have been bred and released into the wild.

Restricted hunting opportunities and stricter hunting laws have allowed the population of Canadian geese in the north to replenish itself, and in many areas populations have thoroughly recovered their numbers.

Top Facts and Information about Flycatchers

Willow flycatcher perched on a tree branch

There are many different types of flycatchers in the world, a very beautiful bird that can be seen in many areas, including both North and Central America. These birds have long captured the attention of birdwatchers and the general population alike. Let's take a look at three of the most well-known flycatchers in the world today.

One of the most common type is the scissor tailed flycatcher, also called a swallowtailed flycatcher. They are part of a group of birds known as Kingbirds and are known for their appetite for insects. A common description of these birds includes pale gray heads, dark gray wings, and long tails that are sometimes forked, especially in the case of the scissortailed species. They can actually grow over a foot in length, and will often nest in shrubs or trees. Dragonflies, grasshoppers, and robber flies are part of their regular diet. They are very similar to a hawk in their attempts to catch these insects, perching at high locations waiting for the insects that fly by.

Another type is the vermilion flycatcher. Although the other flycatcher birds have more basic colors, these are known for their striking dimorphic appearance, usually possessing a very bright red belly and head, with dark brown on their wings and tails. Females will have a peach color instead of red, and the upper side will be dark gray. Although these birds are also found in northern and central America, they have also been spotted in Argentina, South America, and even the Galapagos Islands.

Finally, there is the tyrant flycatcher, a very short variation, especially in comparison to the aforementioned birds. Found in South and North America, there are actually over 400 species of this particular flycatcher, and can blend in well with the foliage due to their gray and brown predominance in color. They are most often found in evergreen forest areas, and can operate well in temperate climates. They are also experts at gleaning insects from bark and leaves, providing them with a large portion of their daily dietary intake. All of these flycatchers are beautiful to behold, each with their own unique characteristics and traits.

The Ins and Outs of Warblers

Black-Throated Blue Dendroica caerulescens

Warblers are fascinating creatures and there is a range of information one can often forget about these animals. Let's take a look at what warblers have to offer. These birds have been around for a long time and they are important.

Genders

The first factor to look at is the variations between the appearances of the two genders. Male and female warblers look different in comparison to one another.

For example, the male will be bright blue and the female is a duller color. The men have a necklace, while the women do not. The men have streaks going across their body, while the women do not.

What Do They Eat?

Warblers have a simple diet and it consists of insects. They hunt for insects and are able to live off them for a long time.

Habitat

Where do warblers live? Most warblers can be found within North America. They can be seen all across the continent, but they are generally visible in Virginia and Southern Missouri.

When winter comes around, the warblers are seen flying off to the nearest warm spot. This warm spot comes in the form of South America.

Reproduction

When do warblers breed? They tend to breed in the months of April and May. They will usually have around 3-4 eggs that are taken care of.

When taking care of their young, warblers will aim to provide them with as many insects as possible. Nests are made in a cup shape consisting of whatever they can find. This usually consists of hair, bark, and grass.

Song:

What kind of noises do warblers tend to make? They are known for their songs and only the males are able to make the noise. It is similar to a buzzing noise in the form of "zzzz".

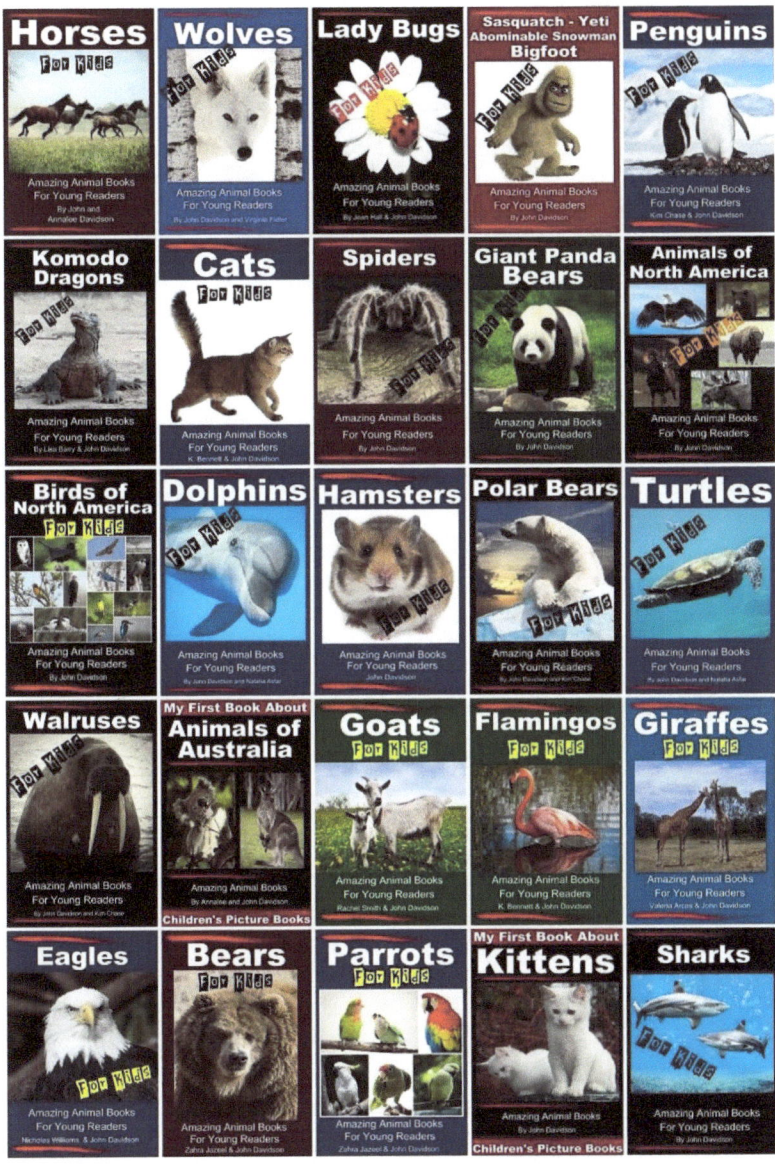

Top Ten Dog Breeds For Kids

Amazing Animal Books For Young Readers

German Shepherds

Dog Books for Kids
K. Bennett

Bulldogs

Dog Books for Kids
K. Bennett

Dachshund

Dog Books for Kids
K. Bennett

Poodles

Dog Books for Kids
K. Bennett

Labrador Retrievers

Dog Books for Kids
K. Bennett

Rottweilers

Dog Books for Kids
K. Bennett

Boxers

Dog Books for Kids
K. Bennett

Golden Retrievers

Dog Books for Kids
K. Bennett

Puppies

Dog Books For Kids

Amazing Animal Books
By John Davidson

Beagles

Dog Books for Kids
K. Bennett

Yorkshire Terriers

Dog Books for Kids
K. Bennett

Dogs
Top Ten Dog Breeds For Kids

Amazing Animal Books For Young Readers
Zahra Jazeel & John Davidson

Cats For Kids

Amazing Animal Books For Young Readers
K. Bennett & John Davidson

Foxes For Kids

Amazing Animal Books For Young Readers
Zahra Jazeel & John Davidson

Wolves For Kids

Amazing Animal Books For Young Readers
By John Davidson and Virginia Fidler

Publisher

JD-Biz Corp

P O Box 374

Mendon, Utah 84325

http://www.jd-biz.com/

Download Free Books!

http://MendonCottageBooks.com

www.ingramcontent.com/pod-product-compliance
Lightning Source LLC
Chambersburg PA
CBHW050818290526

45792CB00001B/166